Author:
Ian Graham studied applied physics at the City University, London. He then took a postgraduate degree in journalism, specialising in science and technology. Since becoming a freelance author and journalist, he has written more than one hundred children's non-fiction books.

Artist:
David Antram was born in Brighton, England, in 1958. He studied at Eastbourne College of Art and then worked in advertising for fifteen years before becoming a full-time artist. He has illustrated many children's non-fiction books.

Series creator:
David Salariya was born in Dundee, Scotland. He has illustrated a wide range of books and has created and designed many new series for publishers in the UK and overseas. He established The Salariya Book Company in 1989. He lives in Brighton with his wife, illustrator Shirley Willis, and their son Jonathan.

Editor: **Stephen Haynes**

Editorial Assistants:
Mark Williams, Tanya Kant

Published in Great Britain in 2008 by
Book House, an imprint of
The Salariya Book Company Ltd
25 Marlborough Place, Brighton BN1 1UB
www.salariya.com
www.book-house.co.uk

HB ISBN-13: 978-1-906370-97-8
PB ISBN-13: 978-1-906370-98-5

© The Salariya Book Company Ltd MMVIII

1 3 5 7 9 8 6 4 2

A CIP catalogue record for this book is available from the British Library.

Printed and bound in China.
Printed on paper from sustainable sources.

Drone Drone Squawk! Oink!

Avoid flying on the Hindenburg!

Written by
Ian Graham

Illustrated by
David Antram

Created and designed by
David Salariya

The Danger Zone

BOOK HOUSE

Contents

Introduction

The year is 1936 – and this is the most exciting day of your life! You have just learned that you are to join the crew of the *Hindenburg* airship. The LZ129 *Hindenburg* is the world's biggest airship. It's as big as an ocean liner, but it's lighter than air, thanks to the hydrogen gas that fills it. It's been built by the Zeppelin company in Germany for luxury flights across the Atlantic Ocean.

You have been working as an airship mechanic for the past five years. Your job is to keep the engines in tip-top condition. At first, you worked in workshops on the ground. Then you flew in the company's smaller airships, looking after the engines during flights. Now, you've been given your dream job in the brand-new *Hindenburg*. It is due to make ten flights from Germany to the United States and seven to Brazil, all in its first year. You'll be going with it – and you can't wait!

I've always dreamed of being a high-flyer.

WHY *HINDENBURG*? The airship is named after Paul von Hindenburg, president of Germany from 1925 to 1934.

WHY HYDROGEN? Many airships are filled with helium gas. But the United States controls the supply of helium and doesn't want to sell it to Germany, so the *Hindenburg* uses hydrogen instead. Hydrogen works just as well as helium, but it does have one disadvantage: it burns easily.

Flying whales

Zeppelin airships have been flying since 1900. They are named after Count Ferdinand von Zeppelin, the German nobleman who developed them. Earlier airships were just big bags of gas; they sometimes collapsed like leaking party balloons. Count Zeppelin's airships are bigger and stronger, because they have a metal frame inside. In 1909 Zeppelin formed Delag, the world's first airline. Its airships have carried tens of thousands of passengers – including you – between German cities. There are military airships, too.

THE FIRST AIRSHIP was built in France by Henri Giffard. It was 44 metres long and powered by a steam engine. On 24 September 1852, Giffard climbed aboard and made the first ever airship flight.

Look out below!

DURING WORLD WAR I (1914–1918), the Germans used airships to drop bombs by hand onto enemy cities.

THERE WERE FEW anti-aircraft guns at this time, but artillerymen could fire at airships by tilting the barrels of their field guns up high.

ZEPPELINS were as big as ocean liners. If they were still flying today, they would dwarf modern airliners like the Boeing 747.

LZ1

LZ129 Hindenburg

Boeing 747 (Jumbo Jet)

RMS Titanic

THE AIRSHIP *AMERICA* tried to fly across the Atlantic Ocean in 1910, but it failed because its engines broke down. The crew and their cat were rescued by a passing British ship, SS *Trent*.

FERDINAND VON ZEPPELIN spent a fortune building his first airship, the LZ1. No-one believed this retired army officer could do it. People were amazed when he succeeded.

Ferdinand von Zeppelin

Building a giant

Reflective coating

Work starts on the *Hindenburg* in autumn 1931. The airship is huge: 245 metres long and 41 metres wide. Workers fit more than 16 kilometres of metal girders together to form the airship's frame. Then 16 enormous drum-shaped bags called gas cells are installed. They hold the hydrogen gas that will lift the giant airship. Finally, the frame is covered with fabric and painted. It is finished by spring 1936.

Gas cells are held in place by a spider's web of netting and bracing wires.

Rudder *steers the airship to port (left) or starboard (right).*

Elevator *helps to move the airship up or down or keep it level.*

Landing wheel *supports the airship when it is on the ground.*

Engine car: *four engines drive the Hindenburg's propellers.*

PAINT JOB. Once the frame is built and the gas cells hung inside it, workers paint the airship's fabric covering with a silver-coloured chemical. The coating reflects the heat of the sun's rays.

Handy hint

Make sure you don't suffer from airsickness!

BIG JOB. The *Hindenburg* is so big that a hangar has had to be built especially for it.

Gas vents let out hydrogen when the airship needs to lose height.

Mooring cone is used to fasten the airship to the mooring mast (see page 22) when it comes in to land.

Keel catwalk *allows the crew to move around the airship.*

Crew quarters

Passenger cabins (see pages 16–17)

Control car (see pages 12–13)

All in a day's work

The *Hindenburg* carries a crew of 61. As well as the captain and officers who command and fly the airship, there are teams of engineers, mechanics and electricians. Meanwhile, cooks, stewards and cabin boys keep the passengers happy.

When you are on duty, you work in one of the four engine cars. Your job is to keep the huge diesel engine running smoothly at the right speed. Officers in the control car send instructions to your engine telegraph, a big round instrument on the wall of the engine car. This tells you the speed to which you need to set the engine.

The crew

FIVE CAPTAINS take turns to command the airship.

THE WATCH OFFICER assists the captains.

NAVIGATORS keep the airship on course.

RADIO OFFICERS make contact with ground stations.

ENGINEERING OFFICERS look after the engines and systems.

THE ELEVATORMAN controls the elevators.

THE HELMSMAN steers the airship.

ELECTRICIANS look after the electrical systems.

ENGINE MECHANICS keep the engines running.

RIGGERS look after the airship's gas cells, bracing wires and netting.

A STEWARDESS joins the crew in 1937.

SEVEN STEWARDS serve the passengers' meals and drinks.

A DOCTOR deals with minor injuries and illnesses.

FIVE COOKS provide freshly cooked meals.

A CABIN BOY helps in the kitchen and does other small jobs.

Handy hint

Protect your ears from the deafening noise of the engine.

Can't hear a thing!

Ah, the glamour of air travel!

INSIDE THE ENGINE CAR, you keep a careful watch on the dials that show the engine's speed and temperature. You must not let the engine overheat, or it could break down.

Flying the giant

One place you love to visit is the control car. Under the airship's nose and with big windows all round, it has a fantastic view. And it's a lot quieter than your engine car! In the control room at the front of the control car, the helmsman steers the airship by turning a wheel. Next to him, the elevatorman turns another wheel to keep the ship level. Behind them in the navigation room, the navigator plots the airship's course. The radio officer works in the radio room, above the control car.

Utility area

Ladder leading to radio room

You won't find any airheads in my crew!

Captain

Navigation room

Landing wheel

YOU ARE HERE

THE RUDDERS (upper and lower) swivel to one side or the other to turn the airship.

THE ELEVATORS swivel up or down to raise or lower the airship's tail.

Elevator wheel

Handy hint

Don't light a match. Leaking hydrogen is extremely flammable – it might catch fire!

THE RADIO OFFICER reports the airship's position and receives weather reports.

Elevatorman

Helmsman

Control room

Rudder wheel

13

Pride of the Reich

The *Hindenburg* is a great German achievement, but at first the Zeppelin company struggled to raise enough money to finish building it. When Adolf Hitler came to power in Germany in 1933, his Nazi government provided the money needed.

One of the first flights you make in 1936 is over the opening ceremony of the Olympic Games in Berlin. The packed Olympic stadium is an amazing sight. Later that year, the *Hindenburg* appears at the Nazi party's annual meeting.

IN RETURN for the Nazi party's funding, the *Hindenburg* has to make propaganda flights for the government, along with its smaller sister-ship, the *Graf Zeppelin*. You wish you didn't have to do this – you don't approve of Hitler's dangerous ideas.

THE SWASTIKA, the cross-shaped emblem of the Nazi party, features on the Hindenburg's *tail fins.*

Handy hint

Learn to like thunderstorms. You're going to get very close to them!

It's raining paper!

At least it's not cats and dogs.

ON ITS FIRST passenger flight to Brazil, the *Hindenburg*'s passengers get a great view of Rio de Janeiro's giant statue of Christ, completed in 1931.

IN MARCH 1936, just before it leaves for Brazil, the *Hindenburg* has to fly across Germany dropping leaflets and blaring out speeches in support of the Nazi government.

15

Inside the Hindenburg

You like walking through the empty airship before the passengers arrive. Everything sparkles and gleams. You have to be careful not to let your oily overalls touch the polished furniture and crisp white tablecloths.

Promenade

> I wish my engine car looked like this...

THE DINING ROOM. Passengers sit at tables set with fine china, silver cutlery and freshly cut flowers.

Gangway

The passengers enter the *Hindenburg* by climbing up two gangways. Once everyone is on board, the gangways fold up into the bottom of the airship. First the passengers come to the lower deck, B-Deck. This is where the kitchen, toilets and shower rooms are. The messrooms where the crew eat their meals are also on this deck. Another flight of stairs takes the passengers up to the bigger A-Deck. This houses the passenger cabins, dining room and lounge.

Dining room

Passenger cabin

THE PASSENGER CABINS are comfortable but small. Each has two beds, one above the other.

Handy hint

Brrr!

Wear warm clothes – it can be freezing cold in the engine cars.

Cutaway view of A-Deck

Lounge

This is the high life!

A SPACIOUS PROMENADE, or walkway, runs along each side of A-Deck, which is lined with big slanting windows.

THE LOUNGE has a huge map of the world on one wall, showing the voyages of great explorers in history.

Flying first class

You couldn't afford to fly on the *Hindenburg* as a passenger. The fare is 400 US dollars for a one-way ticket – about the same price as a car! But then again, the *Hindenburg* is the most spacious and luxurious aircraft ever built. It's simply the best way to see the world's cities, floating just 200–300 metres above the rooftops.

The passengers eat well, too. One of the chefs tells you that the kitchen gets through about 200 kilograms of fresh meat and poultry, 100 kilograms of butter and 800 eggs on a typical Atlantic flight taking less than three days.

I only ever fly first class.

THREE DELICIOUS MEALS a day are served by stewards in the airship's dining room.

THE KITCHEN spreads wonderful cooking smells throughout the airship as the chef prepares the passengers' meals.

THE READING AND WRITING ROOM has a typewriter for passengers to write letters.

Clickety clickety

PASSENGERS enjoy breathtaking views from the promenade windows.

THE LOUNGE PIANO is specially made of aluminium and pigskin to save weight.

EMILIE IMHOFF becomes the first zeppelin stewardess when she joins the *Hindenburg*'s crew for the 1937 season.

The last flight

I t's 3 May 1937, and you are keen to get to work, because the *Hindenburg* is leaving for its first flight of the year to the United States. So far it has flown more than 320,000 kilometres. This will be its 37th transatlantic flight. When you arrive at the new Rhein-Main World Airport near Frankfurt, the *Hindenburg*'s hangar is busy with visitors eager to see the giant airship. Only 36 passengers are making this trip, but the return flight to Germany is due to be full of people travelling to the coronation of King George VI in London.

THE LAST SUPPLIES are loaded early in the morning and final checks are made for the airship's departure in the evening.

Handy hint

Don't wear loose clothing – it might get caught in the machinery.

IN THE LATE AFTERNOON, the *Hindenburg* is walked out of its hangar by the ground crew. Then the passengers begin boarding.

AT 8.15pm you head out along the English Channel and across the Atlantic.

PASSENGERS SPOT the coast of Newfoundland on the third day. They can see icebergs floating in the dark sea.

Squeal!!

Squawk!

WHEN THE *HINDENBURG* appears in the sky over American farms, some of the animals take fright and run about in panic.

PHOTOGRAPHERS in New York's Empire State Building take pictures of the *Hindenburg* as it flies past.

Lakehurst

When you reach the landing ground at Lakehurst, New Jersey, there is a delay of several hours to let a storm pass. At last you hear the order calling the crew to prepare for landing. You can relax for now – you're off duty – but you're due to start work after the landing, preparing the engines for take-off. The captain hopes for a quick turn-round to make up for the delay. Suddenly you hear a strange noise – a kind of muffled thud. Maybe it's the sound of a mooring line snapping? Or is it something more serious?

7.05pm Hindenburg turns at full speed.

Mooring mast

THE *HINDENBURG* hangs motionless in the air. The ground crew gather to pick up the mooring lines so they can pull the giant airship to its mooring mast.

THE FIRST SIGN of trouble noticed by people inside the airship is a bang and a sudden jolt. Everyone is puzzled by it.

I don't like the sound of that...

THUD!

Fire!

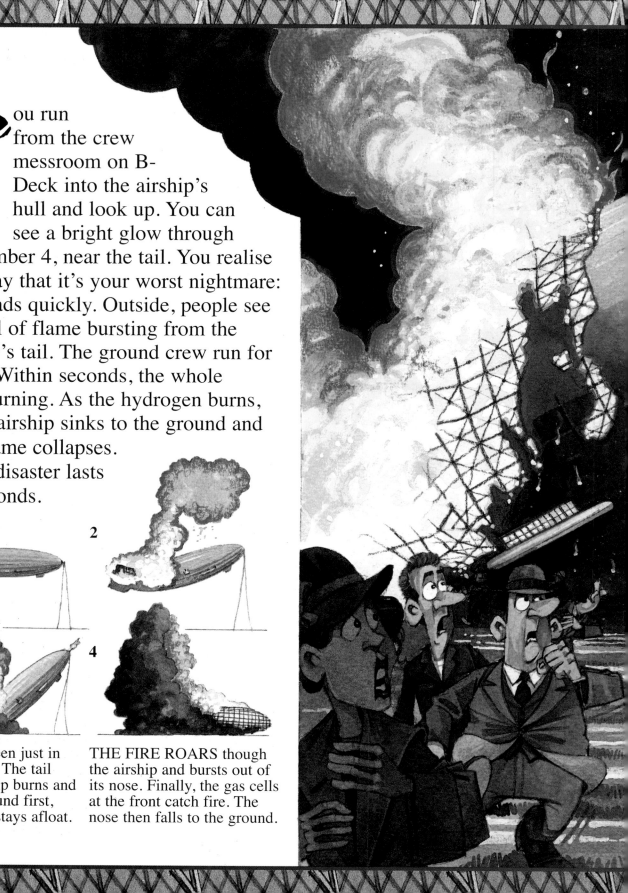

You run from the crew messroom on B-Deck into the airship's hull and look up. You can see a bright glow through gas cell number 4, near the tail. You realise straight away that it's your worst nightmare: fire. It spreads quickly. Outside, people see a bright ball of flame bursting from the *Hindenburg*'s tail. The ground crew run for their lives. Within seconds, the whole airship is burning. As the hydrogen burns, the mighty airship sinks to the ground and its metal frame collapses. The whole disaster lasts only 32 seconds.

FLAMES are seen just in front of the tail. The tail end of the airship burns and sinks to the ground first, while the front stays afloat.

THE FIRE ROARS though the airship and bursts out of its nose. Finally, the gas cells at the front catch fire. The nose then falls to the ground.

Hindenburg

Handy hint

Get to know the escape route you'll use in an emergency.

THE FIRE SPREADS so fast, you have to run to stay ahead of it.

Oh, the humanity!*

RADIO REPORTER Herbert Morrison is recording his description of the landing when he suddenly finds himself reporting the story of his life.

* actual words from Morrison's report

Run!

25

Escape

Inside the *Hindenburg*, the lounge tips up at a crazy angle. Tables and chairs go flying across the floor. Passengers reach for something to hold on to. You climb down as low as you can go inside the hull, staying underneath the raging inferno. When the hull hits the ground, a broken girder rips through the fabric and you are thrown out to safety. Many other people have lucky escapes too. Amazingly, 62 of the 97 people on board survive the disaster.

SOME PASSENGERS desperately jump from windows to get away from the fire. Sadly, many of them die because the airship is still too high above the ground. Most of those who wait survive.

RICHARD KOLLMER, an engine mechanic like you, escapes by ripping open the fabric covering of the tail fin and stepping out through the hole.

IN THE LOUNGE, Margaret Mather pulls her coat around her face. She hears people calling to her from outside. She runs towards the sound of their voices and survives.

Handy hint

Don't panic! Keep calm and try to help others if you can.

My hero!

14-YEAR-OLD cabin boy Werner Franz jumps through a hatch to the ground, but he finds himself trapped amid fire and smoke. Then a water tank bursts above him. The water soaks him, and also clears some of the smoke so he can see his way to safety.

What went wrong?

Everyone is talking about what might have caused the disaster. Some people think the fire may have been started deliberately by a bomb. Like some of the engineers and mechanics, you think a tight turn at full speed may have broken something inside the airship and torn one of the gas cells open. Gas pouring out could have been set on fire by the tiniest spark.

The official inquiry decides that gas leaking from a vent on top of the airship caught fire. Static electricity in the storm clouds – the same kind of electricity that makes lightning – may have caused sparks.

Leaking gas

All I know is I'm lucky to be alive!

FBI AGENTS question some of the crew and passengers, but they cannot find any evidence of crime or terrorism on board the *Hindenburg*.

A PUBLIC INQUIRY begins in a hangar at the Lakehurst Naval Air Station only four days after the disaster.

Crackle!

Mooring mast

Handy hint

Tell the investigators everything you know, so that further disasters like this can be avoided.

Crack!

WAS THE *HINDENBURG* destroyed by a bomb? The bomber might have used a timer, planning to be off the airship by the time the bomb exploded – but the late landing would have trapped the bomber on board. However, the investigators find no trace of a bomb.

DID A BRACING WIRE SNAP and tear open a gas cell? We may never know for sure what brought the *Hindenburg* down.

Glossary

Altitude The height of an aircraft above sea level.

Anti-aircraft guns Guns built specially for shooting at aircraft.

Artillerymen Soldiers who fire big guns, called artillery.

Bracing wires Strong wires that held the *Hindenburg*'s frame in shape.

Catwalk A narrow, raised walkway.

Elevator Part of the tail that tilts up or down to make an airship climb higher, go lower, or stay level.

Elevatorman A crewman who operates the elevator control.

FBI The Federal Bureau of Investigation, the US government's law-enforcement agency.

Field guns Artillery guns mounted on wheels so they can be moved about.

Gas cell A bag full of gas inside an airship.

Gas vents Valves that can be opened like taps to let gas out of the cells.

Girder A strong metal beam.

Hangar A large shelter or building with enough space inside to park one or more aircraft.

Hatch A doorway in a ship, submarine or aircraft.

Helmsman A crewman who operates the helm, or rudder control.

Hull The main body of a ship or airship.

Hydrogen The highly flammable, lighter-than-air gas that filled the *Hindenburg*'s gas cells and lifted the ship into the air.

Keel The strong beam that runs along the bottom of a ship or airship.

LZ Short for *Luftschiff Zeppelin*, German for 'Zeppelin airship'. Every Zeppelin airship had an LZ number. *Hindenburg*'s was LZ129.

Messroom A room where staff or crew eat their meals.

Mooring cone The tip of the airship's nose. When the airship lands, a steel cable from the mooring cone pulls the airship up to a mooring mast fixed to the ground.

Mooring line A rope or cable let down from an airship when it is about to land. The lines are held by people on the ground, or tied to a mooring mast.

Mooring mast A short tower to which an airship is tied when it lands, to hold it steady on the ground.

Navigation Planning and directing the course of a vehicle.

Nazi party The political party that governed Germany from 1933 to 1945.

Propaganda Information that is given out to persuade people to support one point of view or one group of people.

Quarters Rooms or buildings where staff or passengers live.

Reich German for 'empire'. Nazi Germany, 1933–1945, was known as the Third Reich.

Rudder Part of the tail that swivels to one side or the other to steer an airship.

Steward A crew member who looks after passengers and serves their food and drinks.

Vent An opening for releasing gas from an airship. Airships like the *Hindenburg* vented (released) gas in order to reduce height before landing.

Zeppelin A type of airship named after its inventor, Count Ferdinand von Zeppelin.

Index

A
A-Deck 16
America airship 7

B
B-Deck 16, 24
Boeing 747 7

C
cabin boy 10, 27
captain 10
catwalk 9
chef 18
control car 9, 10, 12
control room 12
cook 10
coronation 20
crew 10

D
Delag airline 6
dining room 16
doctor 10

E
electrician 10
elevator 8, 13
elevatorman 10, 12
engine car 10, 11
engine mechanic 10, 26
engine telegraph 10
engineer 10, 28
engineering officer 10

F
FBI 28

G
gangways 16
gas cells 8, 9, 10, 24, 28, 29
Giffard, Henri 6
girders 8, 26
Graf Zeppelin 14
ground crew 21, 22

H
helium 5
helmsman 10, 12
Hindenburg (airship) 5, 8, 14, 15,
  16, 18, 20, 21, 22, 24, 26, 28, 29
Hindenburg, Paul von 5
Hitler, Adolf 14
hull 24
hydrogen 5, 8, 24

I
inquiry 28

K
King George VI 20
kitchen 16, 18

L
Lakehurst, New Jersey 22, 28
lounge 16, 17, 19, 26
LZ1 7
LZ129 5

M
meals 16, 18
mechanic 10, 28
messrooms 16, 24
mooring lines 22, 23
mooring mast 22
Morrison, Herbert 25

N
navigation room 12
navigator 10, 12
Nazi party 14

O
officer 10
Olympic Games 14

P
passenger cabins 16, 17
piano 19
promenade 16, 19

R
radio officer 10, 12, 13
radio room 12
reading and writing room 18
Rhein-Main World Airport 20
rigger 10
rudder 8, 13

S
shower rooms 16
steward 10
stewardess 10, 19
swastika 14

T
ticket price 18
toilets 16

W
watch officer 10
weather reports 13
World War I 6, 7

Z
Zeppelin airships 5, 6, 19
Zeppelin, Count Ferdinand von 7